Fish Sleep But Don't Shut Their Eyes

AND OTHER AMAZING FACTS ABOUT OCEAN CREATURES

by Melvin and Gilda Berger

SCHOLASTIC INC.

New York   Toronto   London   Auckland   Sydney
Mexico City   New Delhi   Hong Kong   Buenos Aires

To Ben, with oceans of love!

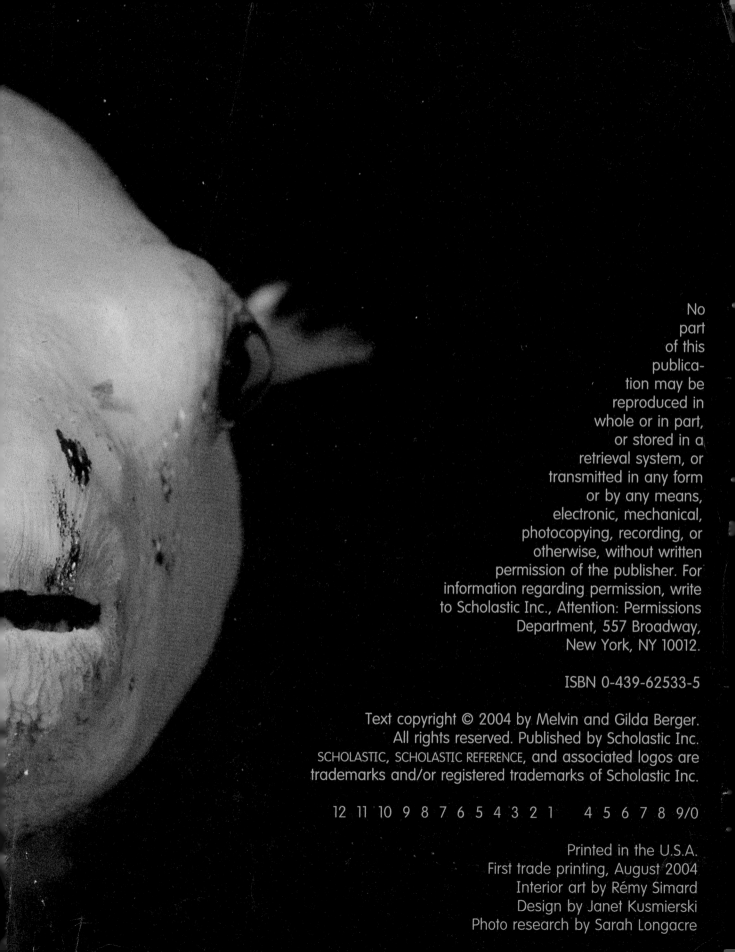

ISBN 0-439-62533-5

12 11 10 9 8 7 6 5 4 3 2 1   4 5 6 7 8 9/0

Printed in the U.S.A.
First trade printing, August 2004
Interior art by Rémy Simard
Design by Janet Kusmierski
Photo research by Sarah Longacre

KEY TO ABBREVIATIONS

cc = cubic centimeter

cm = centimeter

g = gram

kg = kilogram

km = kilometer

kph = kilometers per hour

m = meter

m^3 = cubic meter

mm = millimeter

t = metric ton

INTRODUCTION

Scientists believe that life began in the ocean about four billion years ago. Through the ages, some living things moved from the water to the land. But more forms of life stayed in the water.

Over millions of years, many ocean creatures changed and became more varied. Today, there are a remarkable number of different kinds, or species, of animals in the ocean. In fact, about four out of every five plants and animals on earth live in the ocean!

From the warm tropics to the frigid poles, the oceans are full of life. The waters abound with amazing creatures of every size and shape, from microscopic one-celled protozoans to whales bigger than the largest dinosaurs that ever lived.

Fish Sleep But Don't Shut Their Eyes will take you on a journey into the mysterious ocean. Among the animals you'll read about are:

- flying fish,

- rays that make enough electricity to light a bulb,

- creatures that glow, and

- squids that shoot black "ink."

Dive in and discover the amazing creatures that call the ocean home.

THE WORLD OCEAN

Water, Water Everywhere!

From space, our planet looks blue. That is because oceans cover most of the world's surface and ocean water reflects more of the blue part of the sun's rays than any other color. The Pacific Ocean blankets almost one third of the globe—an area greater than all the land surfaces combined!

The earth has four oceans—Pacific, Atlantic, Indian, and Arctic. But these four oceans flow into one another. Scientists call the joined oceans the *World Ocean*.

Speedy Fact 1

The World Ocean contains 97 percent of all the water on earth.

Speedy Fact 2

Most of the World Ocean lies south of the equator.

Hawaii

Equator

Speedy Fact 3

Much more land is underwater than above the surface.

Speedy Fact 4

If spread evenly over the entire surface of earth, the ocean water would be about 2 miles (3.2 km) deep. A stack of eight Empire State Buildings on the ocean floor would barely reach the surface!

8

The Ocean Bottom

The bottom of the ocean is very rough. Giant mountain chains cover huge stretches of ocean bottom. Huge volcanoes rise up—some so tall that they extend above the water as islands in the sea. In some places, steep valleys, or trenches, sink deep into the ocean floor. The deepest valley in the World Ocean is the Mariana Trench in the Pacific Ocean.

The undersea world is always changing. Melted rocks from deep inside the earth ooze up and form new ocean floor. Under the sea, new islands are always forming.

South Korea
Japan
Northern Marianas
Philippines
Mariana Trench
Indonesia
Papua New Guinea

Speedy Fact 1

A cannonball dropped into the water over the Mariana Trench would take more than an hour to reach the bottom.

Speedy Fact 2

Mount Everest, the world's tallest mountain, could be submerged in the deepest part of the ocean.

Speedy Fact 3

The weight of ocean water creates a pressure at the bottom of the ocean 400 times greater than the pressure at the surface. This pressure could squeeze a wooden block to half its size.

Speedy Fact 4

The deepest water is colder than freezing but stays liquid because it is under pressure.

Speedy Fact 5

Pileups of dead plants and animals on the ocean floor help to form natural gas and oil. But it takes millions of years for the gas and oil to form.

THE OCEAN FOOD CHAIN
What Is a Food Chain?

The ocean food chain is a grouping of living things in which each group feeds on the one below it, and in turn is eaten by the one above it.

Tiny plants grow with light from the sun and chemicals in the water. Animals, including small fish, shellfish, and a few large creatures, feed on the plants. The small animals are then eaten by larger animals, like sharks, tunas, and swordfish. In time, all the animals die. Their decaying bodies return chemicals to the water. The chemicals help the tiny plants to grow.

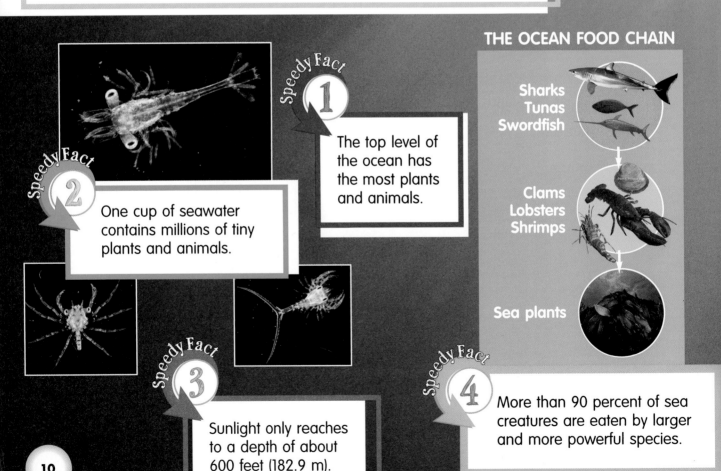

THE OCEAN FOOD CHAIN

Sharks
Tunas
Swordfish

Clams
Lobsters
Shrimps

Sea plants

Speedy Fact 1
The top level of the ocean has the most plants and animals.

Speedy Fact 2
One cup of seawater contains millions of tiny plants and animals.

Speedy Fact 3
Sunlight only reaches to a depth of about 600 feet (182.9 m).

Speedy Fact 4
More than 90 percent of sea creatures are eaten by larger and more powerful species.

Plankton

Plankton are microscopic plants and animals that live in the ocean. They are the most common form of life. These tiny creatures are the food — directly or indirectly—for every living being in the sea.

Animal plankton are slightly larger than plant plankton. One kind of animal plankton, called krill, is the main food for many types of fish, squid, and several kinds of whales. The largest whale, the blue whale, eats about 40 million krill every day.

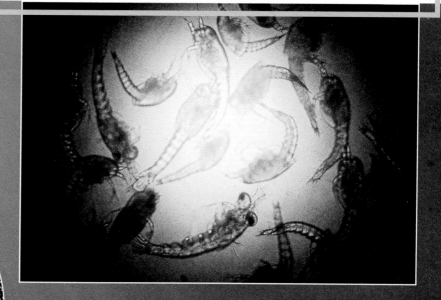

Speedy Fact 1

The word *plankton* comes from the Greek word for "wandering." Moving water carries plant plankton great distances.

Speedy Fact 2

Some kinds of plant plankton glow with an eerie light when they are disturbed.

Speedy Fact 3

The biggest animal plankton is only about a half-inch (1.3 cm) long.

Speedy Fact 4

People make dynamite from the skeletons of animal plankton.

Speedy Fact 5

One cubic foot (0.028 m³) of ocean water may contain 20,000 tiny plant plankton.

LIFE IN THE OCEAN
Animals Without Backbones

Many animals that live in the ocean have no backbones. They are called invertebrates (in-VUR-tuh-brates).

Clams, oysters, octopuses, and squids are a group of invertebrates with soft bodies and no bones. They are known as mollusks (MOL-uhsks). Most mollusks have hard shells, but some do not.

Shrimps, crabs, lobsters, and barnacles are invertebrates with jointed legs and hard outside skeletons. They are called crustaceans (kruhss-TAY-shuhns).

Speedy Fact 1
The giant squid is the world's largest invertebrate. It can be as long as 60 feet (18 m).

Speedy Fact 2
Nine out of every ten animals are invertebrates.

Speedy Fact 3
The smallest invertebrate is a water flea. It is less than 1/24 inch (1 mm) long.

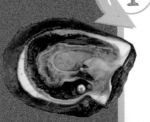

Speedy Fact 4
Mollusks make up the largest group of water animals. Scientists know of about 100,000 different kinds and find another 1,000 new species every year.

Animals With Backbones

Animals with backbones, or spines, are known as vertebrates (VUR-tuh-brates). There are about 40,000 different kinds, including fish, reptiles, and mammals.

Vertebrates are considered more intelligent animals. The backbone of a vertebrate helps protect the main nerve cord, or spinal cord.

Speedy Fact 1

The backbone is made up of many separate, moveable bones. They are strung along the spinal cord like beads on a necklace, letting the animal bend and turn.

Speedy Fact 2

The biggest vertebrate is the blue whale. Its spinal cord is nearly 100 feet (30.5 m) long—about the length of three buses!

Speedy Fact 3

All vertebrates have bodies in which the left and right sides are alike, or *symmetrical*.

Meet the Fish

Fish are vertebrates. They come in many different colors, shapes, and sizes. But they are the same in several ways: All fish have backbones. They hatch from eggs in the water. And they have gills that take oxygen from the water.

There are about 20,000 different kinds of fish in the world. All fish are cold-blooded, which means that their temperature changes with the temperature of the water. Some live in the freezing waters of polar seas. Others make their homes in the warm waters around the equator. Among the best-known fish in the ocean are sharks, tunas, and swordfish.

Speedy Fact 1

The smallest fish is the goby. It's rarely bigger than a fingernail when fully grown.

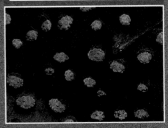

Speedy Fact 2

The 3-inch (7.6 cm) bristlemouth is the most abundant fish. There are billions of bristlemouths living in the ocean.

Speedy Fact 3

Some very small fish live only a few weeks or months. But the large yelloweye rockfish can live to be 118 years old.

Speedy Fact 4

Fish sleep with their eyes open since they don't have eyelids.

Speedy Fact 5

The whale shark is the largest fish. It can grow up to 60 feet (18 m) long and weigh up to 20 tons (22 t).

How Fish Get Food

Fish have many different ways of catching the food they need to live. Certain fish, like the slow-swimming grouper fish, suck in their prey with mouthfuls of water. Species such as barracudas tear the flesh of their victims with their razor-sharp teeth. Electric eels, torpedo rays, and some other fish stun their prey with powerful electric shocks.

Most fish eat other fish, shellfish, and worms. Some are plant eaters. Others live mainly on plankton. And a number are scavengers that feed on waste and the dead bodies of animals.

Speedy Fact 1

The small wrasse swims into the mouths of big fish and eats any bits of food it can find. Surprisingly, the big fish do not seem to mind.

Speedy Fact 2

When they're young, mackerel eat plankton. They switch to small fish as they grow older.

Speedy Fact 3

Pufferfish have beaklike teeth, which they use to crush open the shells of shellfish. A carp does the same job with the teeth in its throat.

Speedy Fact 4

A lamprey has teeth on its tongue, which help it cut into fish and suck up their blood.

Speedy Fact 5

The black swallower has a huge stomach so it can eat fish twice its size.

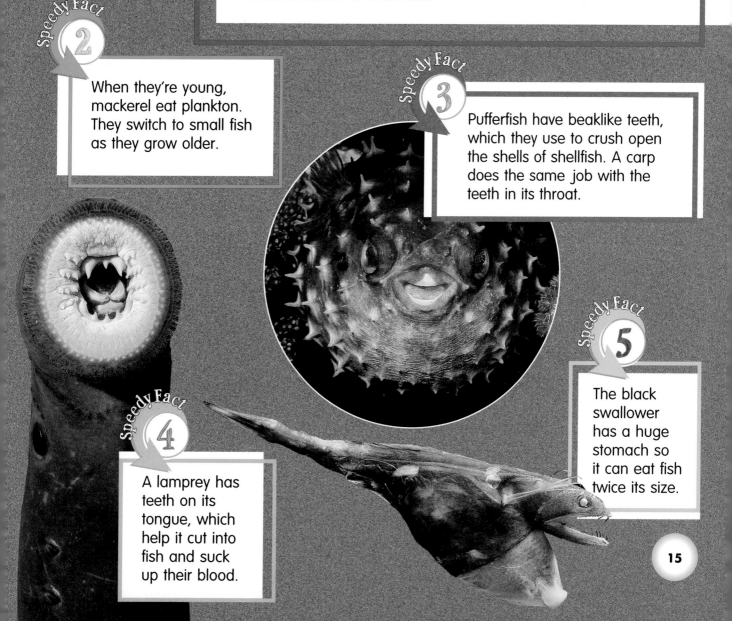

ALONG THE SEASHORE: MOLLUSKS
Clams

Clams usually rest on the ocean floor close to shore. Shallow water is calm and there's lots of food to be found. There are also many places, in the sand or among the rocks, to hide from enemies.

Flowing water passes through the clams' bodies. Clams and other mollusks must keep their bodies moist to stay alive. The clams feed on the tiny bits of plankton that the gills filter out from the water. The food is then digested in their stomachs.

Speedy Fact 1
During low tide, some clams dig holes in the sand with a large muscle called a foot.

Speedy Fact 2
It takes only one second for a razor clam to bury itself in sand.

Speedy Fact 3
A quahog, a type of clam, is believed to live longer than any other ocean creature. Scientists think it may live to the ripe old age of 200.

Speedy Fact 4
The giant clam of the South Pacific is the largest clam. It can be 4 feet (1.2 m) long and weigh 578 pounds (263 kg).

Speedy Fact 5
Some clams of the North Atlantic are smaller than a grain of rice.

AVERAGE LIFE SPAN OF SOME OCEAN CREATURES

Creature	Life span
Quahog clam	200 years
Sea turtle	100 years
Shark	30 years
Tuna fish	13 years
Octopus	2 years

years   20 40 60 80 100 120 140 160 180 200

Oysters

Oysters are like clams. They live close to shore. Their soft bodies are protected by two hard shells. They spend their whole lives in one spot on the ocean floor, usually with their shells slightly open. But when an enemy comes close, they snap their shells shut.

Sometimes a grain of sand slips between the shells and irritates the oyster. Its body produces layers of shell material to cover the grain of sand. This produces a gem known as a pearl.

Speedy Fact 1

A person cannot open an oyster's shells with bare hands.

Speedy Fact 2

A frightened oyster can keep its shell closed for a month or more.

Speedy Fact 3

Oyster eggs hatch about ten hours after the female lays them in the water.

Speedy Fact 4

One female oyster can give birth to about 500 million oysters, called spats, in a year.

Speedy Fact 5

A newborn oyster is no bigger than the head of a pin.

Octopuses

Octopuses live in every ocean of the world. These animals have soft bodies and eight long, flexible arms lined with suckers. Octopuses use their arms to capture prey and pull it to their jaws.

Octopuses move by "jet action." They swim backwards by forcing out a powerful stream of water. When the animals are frightened, they squirt a dark fluid, called ink, into the water. This confuses the attackers—and the octopuses swim away.

Speedy Fact 1

Octopuses range in size from 1 inch (2.5 cm) to more than 20 feet (6 m). They weigh from less than 1 ounce (28 g) to 110 pounds (49.8 kg).

Speedy Fact 2

Octopuses can change their skin color to blend into their surroundings or to hide from enemies. They turn white when scared.

Speedy Fact 3

A female octopus lays grapelike clusters of more than 100,000 eggs at a time. She guards the eggs for two months—without feeding herself.

Speedy Fact 4

The blue-ringed octopus from the coast of Australia is pretty—but deadly. One bite contains enough poison to kill a person.

LENGTHS OF OCTOPUSES

	Blanket (male)	Blue-ringed	Common	Blanket (female)	Apollyon	Giant
feet	.075	.1	6	6.5	28	30
meters	.02	.03	1.8	1.95	8.5	9.1

Scale: 30 (9.1), 25 (7.6), 20 (6), 15 (4.5), 10 (3), 5 (1.5)

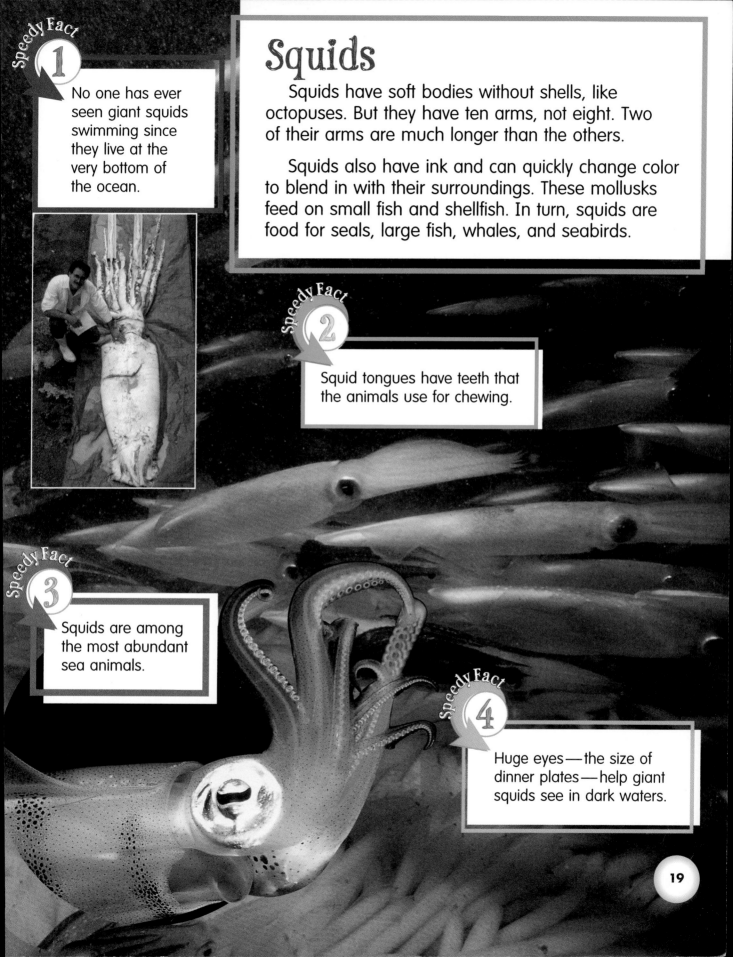

Speedy Fact

1

No one has ever seen giant squids swimming since they live at the very bottom of the ocean.

Squids

Squids have soft bodies without shells, like octopuses. But they have ten arms, not eight. Two of their arms are much longer than the others.

Squids also have ink and can quickly change color to blend in with their surroundings. These mollusks feed on small fish and shellfish. In turn, squids are food for seals, large fish, whales, and seabirds.

Speedy Fact

4

Huge eyes—the size of dinner plates—help giant squids see in dark waters.

CRUSTACEANS
Shrimps

A shrimp's body is surrounded by a stiff shell. As the shrimp gets larger, it sheds its shell and grows a new one. This process is called molting, and it occurs many times during a shrimp's life.

Small shrimps usually feed on plankton. Larger shrimps eat bits of food that drift down to the ocean floor. Shrimps, in turn, are eaten by fish and other water animals.

Speedy Fact 1
Some shrimps eat bits of food that they find in the mouths, gills, and scales of fish.

Speedy Fact 2
Shrimps usually swim forward, but they can flip their tails and swim backward.

Speedy Fact 4
Pistol shrimps snap their claws together to make loud cracking sounds like gunshots. The noise scares away all but the bravest enemies.

Speedy Fact 3
Shrimps come in all colors—gray, brown, white, pink, red, yellow, green, and blue. The peppermint shrimp has stripes and can change colors to blend into the background.

Crabs

Crabs have five pairs of legs. The front pair ends in big claws that the animals use to get food and fight off attackers. Most crabs scurry along sideways on the tips of the other four pairs of legs, looking for bits of food on sandy beaches or muddy shores. On crabs that swim, the last pair of legs has flat, paddlelike tips.

Crabs breathe with their gills. The gills take oxygen from the water. Then they squirt out the water through two small holes on the roofs of their mouths.

Crabs come in many sizes. The smallest crab is the gall crab, which is only one tenth of an inch (2.5 mm) wide. The largest crab, the giant spider crab, is nearly 2,000 times bigger. It stretches 12 feet (3.7 m) across.

Speedy Fact 1

Male crabs have bigger claws than female crabs.

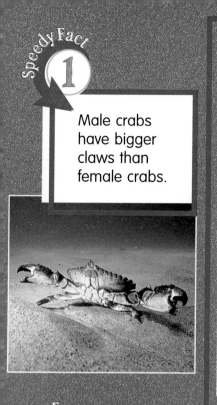

Speedy Fact 2

If an enemy catches a crab by a leg, part of the leg snaps off. In a few months, the missing part grows back—but usually smaller than the original.

Speedy Fact 3

The hermit crab has no shell of its own. It lives in shells discarded by other animals.

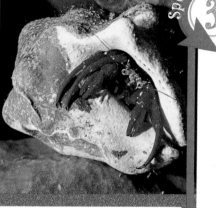

Speedy Fact 4

The male fiddler crab got its name from the way it waves its one gigantic claw back and forth—like someone playing a fiddle.

Speedy Fact 5

To hide themselves, spider crabs and decorator crabs stick pieces of seaweed to the tops of their shells.

Lobsters

Most lobsters have two front claws that are almost as long as their bodies. One of the claws is thick and heavy with big, strong teeth to crush prey. The other claw is smaller and has sharp teeth to pull the prey apart.

During the day, lobsters hide in sand or under rocks along the seacoast. At night, lobsters walk along the ocean bottom looking for food—mostly crabs, small fish, other lobsters, and dead animals. Their waving feelers sense nearby prey. Also, a lobster's shell is covered with millions of tiny hairs that sense chemicals in the water and help it find food. Lobsters grab food with their claws.

Speedy Fact 1
A lobster may molt 15 times in its first year. While the fresh shell grows hard—in about 15 minutes—the lobster hides in the sand.

Speedy Fact 4
A lobster caught off the coast of Canada was a record 3.5 feet (1 m) long.

Speedy Fact 2
A lobster's eyes are at the end of two long, slender organs called stalks—not on its head!

Speedy Fact 3
A lobster's body has 19 parts—five in its head; eight in its thorax, or center section; and six in its abdomen, or back.

Speedy Fact 5
Some lobsters are "right-handed;" others are "left-handed."

Speedy Fact 6
Lobsters, which usually have blue or green shells, turn bright red when cooked.

Barnacles

Barnacles each have one eye and three pairs of legs at birth. As they grow, they get two more eyes, three more pairs of legs, and two large feelers. Full-grown barnacles lose their eyes and cement themselves to rocks, ship bottoms, piers, whales, or other underwater objects. Here they stay for the rest of their lives.

An adult barnacle has a hard, volcano-shaped shell. The top is usually open but slams shut in case of danger. Six pairs of feathery legs wave in the water outside the shell to capture any plankton that floats by.

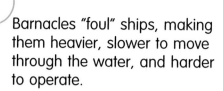

Speedy Fact 1

Barnacles "foul" ships, making them heavier, slower to move through the water, and harder to operate.

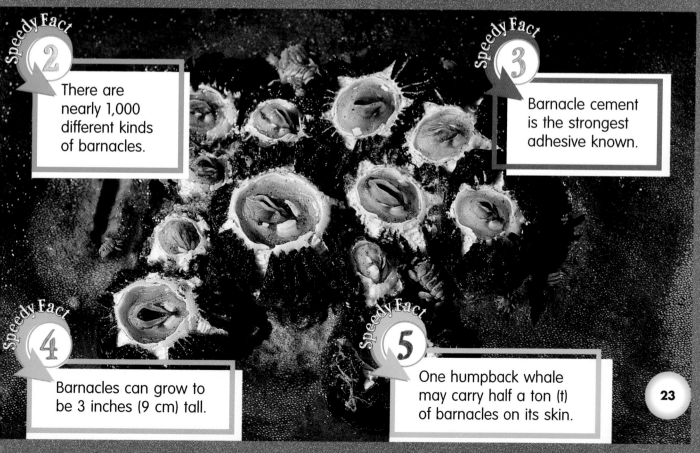

Speedy Fact 2

There are nearly 1,000 different kinds of barnacles.

Speedy Fact 3

Barnacle cement is the strongest adhesive known.

Speedy Fact 4

Barnacles can grow to be 3 inches (9 cm) tall.

Speedy Fact 5

One humpback whale may carry half a ton (t) of barnacles on its skin.

REPTILES
Sea Turtles

Sea turtles are among the few reptiles that live in the ocean. Reptiles are vertebrates with a skin of scales or plates. All reptiles have lungs and breathe air.

Sea turtles have long flippers instead of short legs like land turtles. Also, they cannot pull their head and limbs into their hard shells.

Male sea turtles spend all their time in the water. But females come out of the water to lay their eggs on the beaches where they were born.

Speedy Fact 1

Ridley turtles are the smallest sea turtles. They reach a full size of no more than 28 inches (71.1 cm).

Speedy Fact 2

The Pacific leatherback turtle got its name from the thick, leathery skin on its top shell.

Speedy Fact 3

Sea turtles seem to cry when they come ashore. The tears are probably to wash sand from their eyes.

Speedy Fact 4

The leatherback swims about 22 miles per hour (35.4 kph). A fast human swimmer can swim only about 12 miles per hour (19.3 kph).

Speedy Fact 5

The hawksbill turtle is an endangered animal. Hunters catch and kill huge numbers for the turtles' beautiful shells.

Ascension Island

Green Turtles

The green turtle is large—up to 5 feet (1.5 m) long. It lives in the warm waters of both the Atlantic and Pacific oceans. Even though it is called a green turtle, its shell is brown.

The most fascinating green turtles live off the coast of Brazil in South America. Every two or three years they start swimming across the Atlantic Ocean. They migrate more than 1,250 miles (2,011.5 km). Their journey takes them to tiny Ascension Island in the middle of the Atlantic. Here, they lay eggs on the very beach on which they were born. Then they return to Brazil.

Speedy Fact 1

Like other turtles, green turtles have no teeth. A sharp, jagged edge on their lower jaw cuts through tough food.

Speedy Fact 2

Young green turtles eat jellyfish and small sea animals. As they grow older, the green turtles switch to sea grass and other plants.

Speedy Fact 3

Female green turtles lay about 100 eggs at a time, but usually just one survives.

Sea Snakes

Sea snakes are ocean-dwelling reptiles, just like sea turtles. They are very poisonous. Their poison is much stronger than the poison of land snakes. Sea snakes breathe air and mostly live in the warm waters of the Pacific and Indian oceans. None are found in the Atlantic.

Sea snakes are flat, not round. They usually swim in shallow, coastal waters. Sometimes a huge group of sea snakes may be spotted in the open ocean. Scientists think they may have been carried there by ocean currents.

Speedy Fact 1
Sea snakes can stay underwater no longer than two hours before they must come up to breathe.

Speedy Fact 2
The main food of sea snakes is small fish swimming around coral reefs.

Speedy Fact 3
Sea snakes can swim forward or backward.

Speedy Fact 4
Sea snakes have nostrils on top of their snouts. This allows them to breathe with their head underwater. When diving, the snakes can seal their nostrils so no water gets in.

Speedy Fact 5
Most sea snakes give birth in the water to living snakes.

Sea Kraits

You can recognize a sea krait by the bright dark and white bands that cover its entire body. Even though they are sea snakes, sea kraits spend lots of time ashore on small islands. Here, they warm themselves in the sun and lay eggs, often in caves above the tide line.

Sea kraits are longer than most sea snakes, some reaching 5 feet (1.5 m). Their bodies are round throughout, except for the flat, paddlelike tail for swimming. The large scales under the belly help them crawl on land.

Speedy Fact
1
Sea kraits have a good sense of taste. Their taste buds are on the roof of the mouth and along their teeth.

Speedy Fact
2
The favorite foods of sea kraits are eels and fish eggs.

Speedy Fact
3
Although their poison is very powerful, sea kraits rarely use it, even when being attacked.

Speedy Fact
4
Of the six kinds of sea kraits, five live in warm ocean waters and one lives in a freshwater lake in the Solomon Islands.

CORAL REEF
What Is a Coral Reef?

A coral reef is a structure that forms in warm, shallow seas. There are coral reefs around all continents except Europe and Antarctica. A coral reef is made up of the skeletons of tiny animals called coral polyps, which are soft-bodied little animals related to jellyfish.

Polyps have tentacles that they use to get food from the water. When the polyps die, their stony skeletons pile up and form the reef. Colonies of new polyps grow on the remains. They make green, purple, orange, and yellow corals shaped like branches, fans, brains, or horns.

Speedy Fact 1
The best-known reef, Australia's Great Barrier Reef, is more than 1,000 miles (1,600 km) long. The largest living structure on earth, this reef can be seen from outer space.

Speedy Fact 2
Most coral reefs grow only about a half-inch (1.3 cm) a year.

Speedy Fact 3
Some coral reefs rise above the water level and form coral islands.

Speedy Fact 4
One kind of coral, dead man's fingers, looks like the fingers of a corpse.

Speedy Fact 5
The crown-of-thorns starfish hurts the coral reef because it feeds on the coral.

At Home on a Coral Reef

Coral reefs are home to more different kinds of sea creatures than any other part of the ocean. In fact, about one out of every three kinds of ocean fish lives on a coral reef. The Great Barrier Reef alone has 400 species of coral polyps, 1,500 species of fish, and many different kinds of crabs, clams, eels, snails, and other sea animals.

Many of the creatures that live in, on, or around a coral reef are small, which helps them fit between the rocks. Their bright colors make the animals hard to see against the colorful reef.

Speedy Fact 1
Sea anemones capture small fish or shrimps with their poisonous tentacles. Only the clown fish is not hurt by the anemone's poison.

Speedy Fact 2
Starfish have from 5 to 40 arms. If a starfish loses an arm, it grows a new one.

Speedy Fact 3
A scientist once counted 17,000 tiny worms, crabs, and fish living inside a single, large reef-dwelling sponge.

Speedy Fact 4
The parrotfish is one of the noisiest fish on the reef. It makes a loud, scraping sound when feeding on coral.

Speedy Fact 5
When in danger, the pufferfish blows itself up like a balloon so it can't be swallowed by other fish.

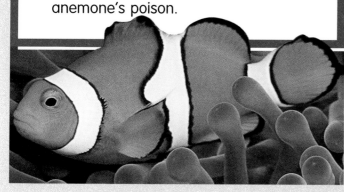

THE OPEN OCEAN: SHARKS

Meet the Sharks

Today, scientists know about 370 different kinds of sharks. They are among the oldest creatures on earth. Sharks have been on earth for about 350 million years—long before the time of the dinosaurs. The most ancient known shark, the megalodon, lived from about 50 million years ago until it became extinct 12,000 years ago. Scientists believe this giant shark was about 50 feet (15.2 m) long and weighed 28,000 pounds (12,700.8 kg).

Sharks live in every ocean of the world. A few swim in water so shallow that their backs and fins stick up out of the water. Others are found only in the deepest parts of the ocean, as far as 2 miles (3.2 km) below the surface.

Speedy Fact 1

The Japanese name of the dwarf shark, *tsuranagakobitozame*, is almost as long as the shark itself. The word means "a dwarf shark with a long face."

Speedy Fact 2

The stomach of a tiger shark caught near the Philippines held nine shoes, a belt, and a pair of pants.

Speedy Fact 3

In 1993, a bull shark wandered into the freshwater Hudson River and was not far from Times Square in New York City.

Speedy Fact 4

The hammerhead shark gets the prize for strangest looks. Its eyes are located at the ends of a 3-foot (0.9 m) bar across its head.

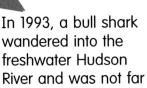

30

The Body of a Shark

Sharks differ from most other fish in a couple of ways. First, sharks do not have bones like other fish. A shark's skeleton is made of bendable cartilage, like the tip of your nose and your ears. Second, shark skin is usually covered with tiny, sharp teeth like a coat of nails, not scales.

Sharks feed on every living creature in the sea, from the weakest to the most powerful. Their mouths are lined with thousands of very sharp teeth. Worn teeth are constantly falling out. But all sharks have many extras. As soon as one tooth falls out, another moves up to take its place. A shark may grow as many as 30,000 teeth in its lifetime.

Speedy Fact 1

After eating a large sea creature, the great white shark starts looking for its next meal. Still, the animal can go three months without a bite to eat.

Speedy Fact 2

Ancient Greeks burned shark teeth and rubbed the ashes on their gums to relieve toothaches.

Speedy Fact 3

The juices in a shark's stomach are strong enough to dissolve metal.

Speedy Fact 4

Some sharks can bite with a force of about 132 pounds (60 kg)—strong enough to cut through steel.

Speedy Fact 5

Sailors once used shark teeth for shaving.

SHARKS' LENGTHS

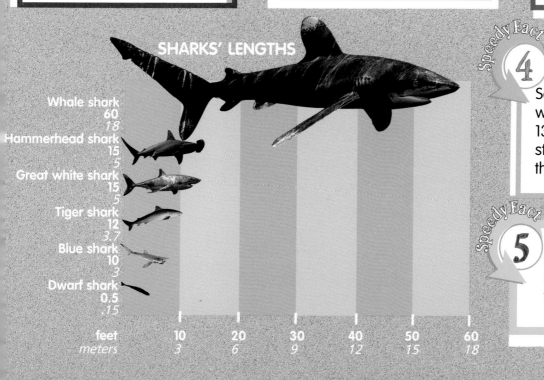

Whale shark
60
18

Hammerhead shark
15
5

Great white shark
15
5

Tiger shark
12
3.7

Blue shark
10
3

Dwarf shark
0.5
.15

feet	10	20	30	40	50	60
meters	*3*	*6*	*9*	*12*	*15*	*18*

Shark Senses

Sharks have especially sharp senses. People call them "swimming noses," because two thirds of a shark's brain is devoted to the sense of smell. Their vision is excellent, too. Sharks can see as well near the sunny ocean surface as they can in the darkest parts of the sea.

A shark's ears are two tiny holes in the skin, just behind their eyes. Yet sharks can pick up the softest sounds. A lateral line along the shark's sides, just beneath the skin, lets sharks feel vibrations in the water and swim into action!

Speedy Fact 1
Sharks can smell a drop of blood 2 miles (3.2 km) away. The shark's nostrils are for smelling, not breathing.

Speedy Fact 2
Sharks can hear a fish swimming at a distance of a half-mile (0.8 km).

Speedy Fact 3
Sharks can see about 10 times better than humans.

Speedy Fact 4
Deepwater sharks have especially big eyes; the thresher shark's eyes are the size of human fists.

Speedy Fact 5
Sharks can detect the tiniest amount of electricity given off by a living sea creature.

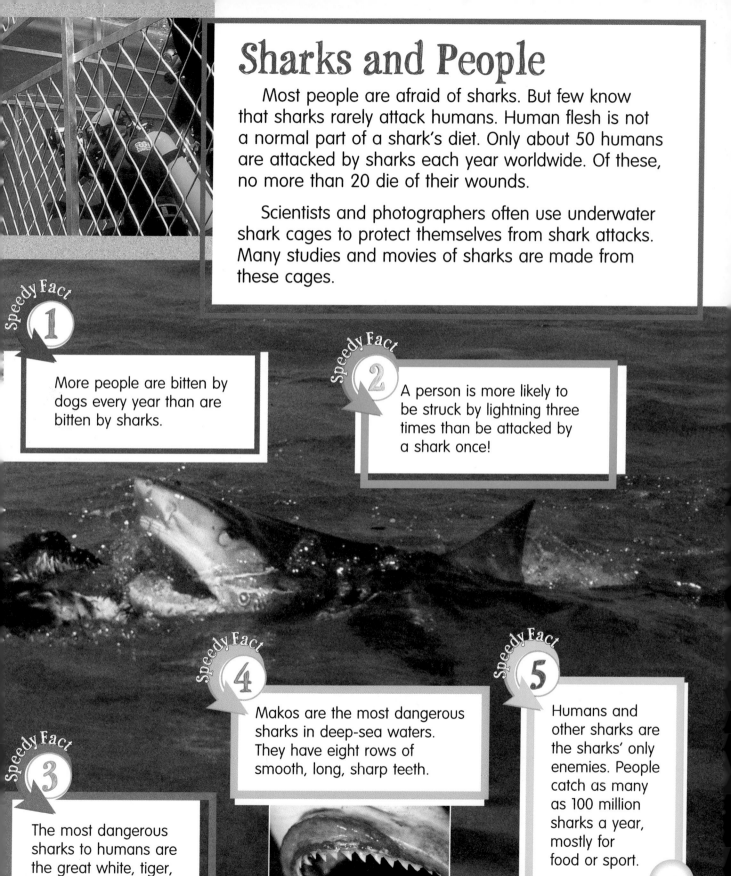

Sharks and People

Most people are afraid of sharks. But few know that sharks rarely attack humans. Human flesh is not a normal part of a shark's diet. Only about 50 humans are attacked by sharks each year worldwide. Of these, no more than 20 die of their wounds.

Scientists and photographers often use underwater shark cages to protect themselves from shark attacks. Many studies and movies of sharks are made from these cages.

Speedy Fact 1

More people are bitten by dogs every year than are bitten by sharks.

Speedy Fact 2

A person is more likely to be struck by lightning three times than be attacked by a shark once!

Speedy Fact 4

Makos are the most dangerous sharks in deep-sea waters. They have eight rows of smooth, long, sharp teeth.

Speedy Fact 5

Humans and other sharks are the sharks' only enemies. People catch as many as 100 million sharks a year, mostly for food or sport.

Speedy Fact 3

The most dangerous sharks to humans are the great white, tiger, and bull sharks.

LARGE FISH
Tuna Fish

About 90 percent of all ocean animals, including tuna fish, live in the upper level of the sea, far from the shore. This area extends down about 600 feet (180 m) from the surface—about as far as the sun's light reaches.

Tunas are among the fastest fish. Some tuna fish can reach speeds of 50 miles per hour (80 kph). Like most other fish, a tuna breathes through gills. But unlike the vast majority of fish, a tuna cannot pump water over its gills. It must keep swimming in order to get oxygen from the water.

Speedy Fact 1

Tunas range in size from the big northern blue fin, which can be 14 feet (4.3 m) long and weigh 1,600 pounds (725.7 kg), to the tiny bullet tuna at a length of 20 inches (51 cm) and weighing 5 pounds (2.3 kg).

Speedy Fact 2

One blue fin tuna crossed the Atlantic Ocean in 119 days— an average of about 25 miles (40.3 km) a day.

Speedy Fact 3

Tunas can swim from one ocean to another.

Speedy Fact 4

Scientists estimate a tuna swims about 1 million miles (1.6 million km) in its lifetime.

The swordfish's sword is about half the length of its body.

Swordfish

Swordfish are large, open-sea fish with long, rounded bodies and large eyes. These fish take their name from the "sword," their long, stiff, flat upper jaw. Often more than 1 yard (1 m) long, the sword is sharp enough to cut through the side of a wooden boat.

At night, swordfish swim in the upper levels of the ocean. During the day, they tend to stay deeper in the water. The fish uses its sword to catch squids, herrings, mackerels, and other fish that travel in large groups, called *schools*.

The swordfish is a fast swimmer. It can slice through the water at 55 miles per hour (88 kph).

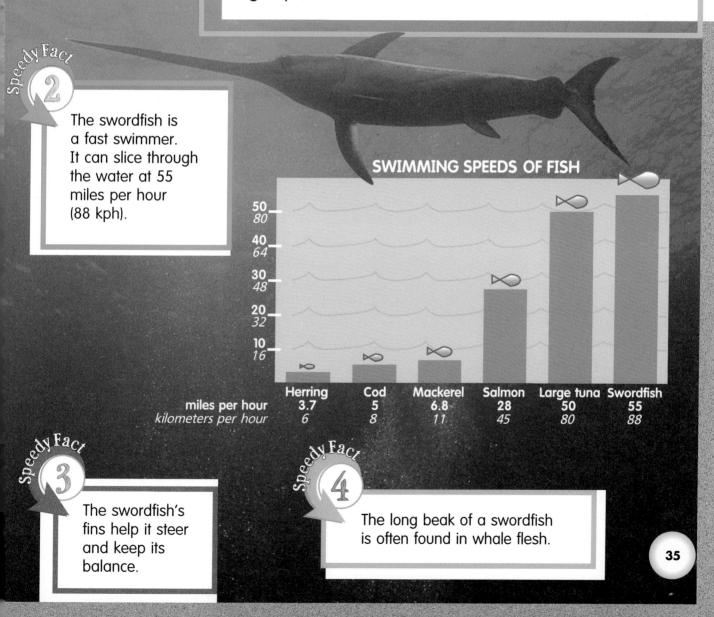

SWIMMING SPEEDS OF FISH

	Herring	Cod	Mackerel	Salmon	Large tuna	Swordfish
miles per hour	3.7	5	6.8	28	50	55
kilometers per hour	6	8	11	45	80	88

The swordfish's fins help it steer and keep its balance.

The long beak of a swordfish is often found in whale flesh.

Flying Fish

Flying fish live in warm seas. They lift themselves out of the water by beating the surface with their powerful tails. The fish then glide through the air on their large, spread-out fins, which act like wings. By wiggling their bodies and bending their tail fins, the fish control the direction in which they are flying.

There are more than 50 different kinds of flying fish. A typical flying fish, the California flying fish, is about 18 inches (46 cm) long.

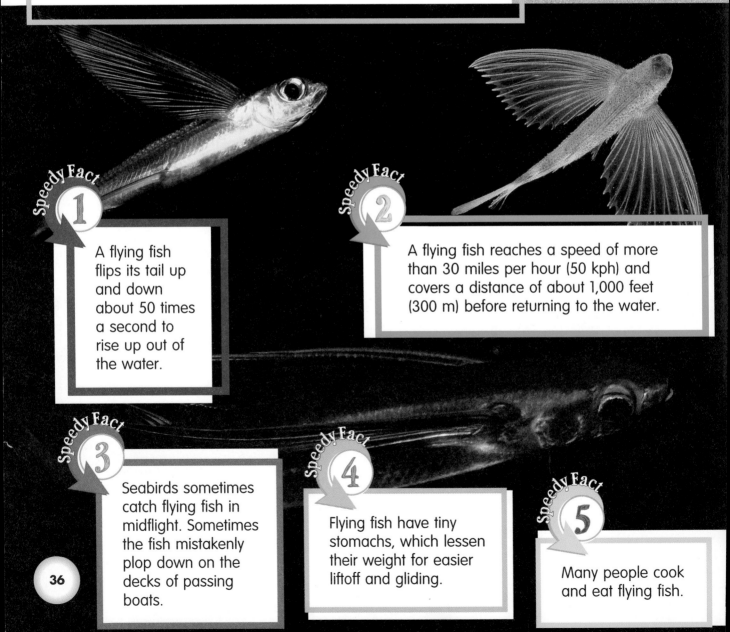

Speedy Fact 1
A flying fish flips its tail up and down about 50 times a second to rise up out of the water.

Speedy Fact 2
A flying fish reaches a speed of more than 30 miles per hour (50 kph) and covers a distance of about 1,000 feet (300 m) before returning to the water.

Speedy Fact 3
Seabirds sometimes catch flying fish in midflight. Sometimes the fish mistakenly plop down on the decks of passing boats.

Speedy Fact 4
Flying fish have tiny stomachs, which lessen their weight for easier liftoff and gliding.

Speedy Fact 5
Many people cook and eat flying fish.

Manta rays can be as long as 22 feet (6.7 m), as wide as 29 feet (8.8 m), and weigh as much as 3,000 pounds (1,360.8 kg).

Manta Rays

Manta rays feed mostly on plant and animal plankton found at the surface of the sea. The fish use the two stiff fins on the front of their bodies to funnel the plankton-rich water into their mouths.

Manta rays are like sharks. They have boneless, flexible skeletons of cartilage and they breathe through body openings called gill slits. To swim, the flat, wide-bodied rays flap their large fins up and down in a gentle, waving motion.

Speedy Fact
2

When chased, a manta ray sometimes jumps up out of the water.

Speedy Fact
3

Female manta rays sometimes give birth while leaping out of the water.

JELLYFISH
Meet the Jellyfish

Jellyfish are invertebrates that take their name from the jellylike material in their bodies. They have no heart, bones, brain, or eyes. Some kinds are no larger than a pea. Others may be as big as 7.8 feet (2.4 m) across, with 120-foot (36.6 m) long poisonous threads, or tentacles, hanging below.

Much of the time, jellyfish float in the water and are moved by tides, currents, and winds. But they can also swim by opening and closing their umbrellalike bodies.

Speedy Fact 1

A jellyfish's tentacles shoot out tiny poison darts that capture the prey and pop it into the animal's mouth.

Speedy Fact 2

The venom of the Australian box jellyfish is stronger than a cobra's venom and can kill a person in minutes.

Speedy Fact 3

The purple jellyfish may be yellow, red, or brown in color.

Speedy Fact 4

A sea wasp is a kind of jellyfish with a long, trunklike mouth. It can swim as fast as a good human swimmer.

Speedy Fact 5

Without food, a 1-foot (30 cm) long jellyfish can shrink down to about an inch (2.5 cm).

Portuguese Man-of-War

The Portuguese man-of-war looks like a jellyfish but is really hundreds of separate creatures living together. One group floats on top; the second group forms the hanging tentacles; the third group digests the food; and the fourth group lays eggs.

The Portuguese man-of-war cannot swim. It makes a special gas that inflates a float in its body. Then it is moved around by winds that push this gas-filled float. The poison of a Portuguese man-of-war is deadly to almost all fish. It also wounds any humans who touch it.

Speedy Fact 1

Each tentacle of a Portuguese man-of-war, which may be 30 feet (10 m) long, is a whole animal.

Speedy Fact 2

Shepherdfish

Only two fish—the shepherdfish and the ocean sunfish—are not harmed by the Portuguese man-of-war.

Speedy Fact 3

The poison of a Portuguese man-of-war is dangerous, even after the animal dies and washes up on a beach.

Speedy Fact 4

Ocean sunfish

Sailors named the Portuguese man-of-war after a type of sailing ship popular long ago.

SEA MAMMALS
Meet the Whales

Whales are mammals, like dolphins, dogs, cats, lions, tigers, and humans. Mammals give birth to live babies and nurse the babies with milk from the mother's body. They are also warm-blooded. This means their temperature stays about the same no matter how warm or cold the water.

Most whales have between 2 and 50 teeth. These are called toothed whales. The rest have long, thin plates, called baleen, instead of teeth. Baleen is made of the same kind of material as your fingernails. The baleen in their mouths traps tiny fish or plankton from the water.

Speedy Fact 1

Narwhals have only two teeth, but in the males one tooth is a 9-foot (2.7 m) long tusk that juts straight out of its mouth.

Speedy Fact 2

Each tooth in a sperm whale's jaw weighs more than half a pound.

Speedy Fact 3

Bowhead whales have the longest baleen of all baleen whales—as long as 15 feet (4.6 m). Laid end to end, the plates would stretch over a mile (1.6 km).

Speedy Fact 4

Toothed whales do not chew their food. They swallow fish, squid, or other food whole.

surface	57° 13.8°
2000 609.6	43° 6.1°
6000 1828.8	36° 2.2°
10000 3048	35° 1.7°
14000 4267.2	34° 1.1°
feet meters	°Fahrenheit °Celsius

The Body of a Whale

Fossils of whale ancestors show that they once lived on land. They were huge beasts, probably covered with fur, and walked on four legs. When these animals moved into the sea, their front legs gradually developed into flippers for steering and keeping their balance. Their rear legs slowly disappeared.

Whales now are well fit for life in the ocean. They have smooth, rubbery skin that easily slips through the water. Under the skin is a thick layer of fat, called blubber, that helps keep them warm in cold water.

Speedy Fact 1

Blue whales are the biggest animals that ever lived. Their hearts are as big as small automobiles.

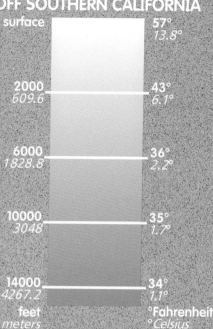

Speedy Fact 2

A nursing baby blue whale gains about 10 pounds (4.5 kg) every hour!

Speedy Fact 3

The sound made by a blue whale is 500 times louder than the loudest sound a human can make.

Speedy Fact 4

A whale's ears are just two small holes in its skin, yet it can hear sounds from 1,000 miles (1,609 km) away.

Speedy Fact 5

A whale's skin can be 14 inches (35.6 cm) thick. Its blubber may be 2 feet (60.9 cm) thick.

41

Meet the Dolphins

Dolphins are close relatives of whales. Like whales, dolphins are mammals, but most dolphins are smaller than most whales. Dolphins mostly swim in upper ocean waters. Yet they can dive as deep as 1,000 feet (304.8 m) and leap as high as 20 feet (6.1 m) above the water.

Dolphins have long been part of people's lives. Ancient Greeks believed dolphins were sacred animals. Sailors used to say that dolphins swimming near a ship brought good luck. And, over many years, experts have trained these smart animals to perform in movies, on television shows, and at aquariums and water parks.

Speedy Fact 1
The oldest dolphin on record reached the age of 32.

Speedy Fact 2
Dolphins have 200 or more teeth for grabbing prey. But they don't chew their food.

Speedy Fact 3
Dolphins sleep with half their brain still alert for danger.

Speedy Fact 5
Dolphins make clicking sounds as they swim. The length of time it takes the echo to return helps them locate fish or other objects in the water. This is called *echolocation*.

Speedy Fact 4
Dolphins sometimes save people in the ocean, probably because they mistake the people for other dolphins in trouble.

42

Dolphin Families

Newborn dolphins, called calves, are born in the spring or early summer—tail first. Quickly, the mother pushes the calf to the surface to take its first breath of air. The newborn calf is about one third the length of its mother.

The mother feeds the baby with milk from her body every 15 minutes, all day long, for a year or more. By one year of age, the calf is ready to find its own food.

Speedy Fact 1

Dolphin babies don't cry—it just looks that way. Covering their eyes is a special liquid that looks like tears.

Speedy Fact 2

Mother dolphins sometimes spank their babies with their flippers.

Speedy Fact 3

The father swims near the mother and calf but does not help to care for the youngster.

Speedy Fact 4

When dolphins are about eight years old, they are ready to have calves of their own.

THE DEEP SEA AND OCEAN FLOOR: LIFE IN THE DARK

Fish With Big Mouths

Fish that live at the bottom of the deep, dark sea have a hard time finding food. Many live on bits of food that drift down from above. Some hunt one another.

Deep-sea fish, such as gulper eels and viperfish, have extra-large mouths. They swim with their giant mouths open to scoop up any prey that appears in the water.

Speedy Fact 1

Viper fish have hinged jaws that swing far apart. They can swallow prey twice their size!

Speedy Fact 2

When the great swallower overeats, the skin on its stomach stretches so thin that you can see its last meal.

Speedy Fact 3

The gulper eel is almost all mouth with a long, thin tail.

Speedy Fact 4

From about 600 feet (183 m) below the surface to the ocean bottom, it is completely dark. Deep waters are also freezing cold—about 32° degrees Fahrenheit (0°C).

Animals That Stay in One Place

A small number of deep-ocean creatures, such as tubeworms and sea pens, do not swim or move about. Instead, they stay in one place on the ocean floor. They wait for their food to be delivered to them by the flowing water.

Tubeworms have long, thin bodies with bright red heads. They live inside white tubes, as tall as adult men, stuck to the oceanfloor. The tubes protect them from crabs and other enemies. Sea pens are beautiful animals that look like old-fashioned quills or feather pens.

Speedy Fact 1

Tubeworms never eat. They get all their food from germs that live in their bodies.

Speedy Fact 2

The sea pen is not one animal, but a group of many individual animals living together.

Speedy Fact 3

If anything touches a sea pen, the sea pen lights up and glows.

47

THE FUTURE OF THE OCEANS

The world ocean is one of science's last frontiers. Scientists called marine biologists are trying to unravel the many mysteries that surround life in the sea.

Marine biologists have many special projects. Some go out on research ships, observing and gathering samples of ocean life around the world. Others work in shore laboratories, studying different sea creatures.

In one study, marine biologists are experimenting with the effects of pollution on animal growth. In another, scientists are looking at ways to protect species from becoming extinct, due to people taking too many fish from the sea. Still other scientists are trying to improve fish farms, raising sea creatures the way ranchers raise cattle.

Marine biologists are dedicated to improving life in the sea. The future of the oceans depends on these scientists and on all of us.